decadent
SHAKES
milkshakes with more

We dedicate this book to all those who have shared a smile,
a laugh or a memory with us along the way!

Enjoy and love life,
Matt, Sarah and Brendo.

decadent SHAKES

milkshakes with more

MATTHEW, SARAH & BRENDAN AOUAD

NEW
HOLLAND

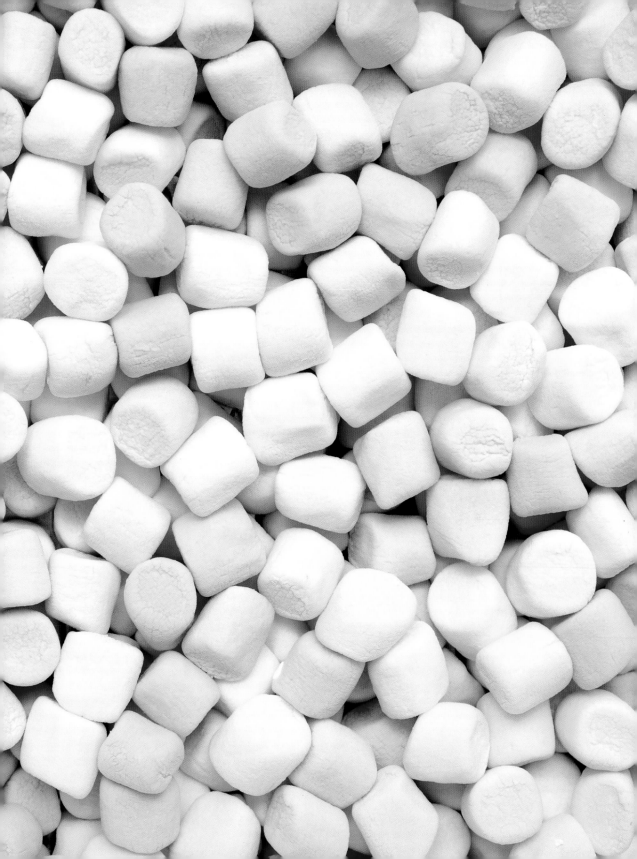

CONTENTS

Introduction 8
Notes About Safety 11
Decorating Your Glass 13
Fruity Mania 15
Chocolate Mania 31
Super Sweet 63
Crazy Cool 89
Glossary 106
Index 108

INTRODUCTION

The Vogue Café has been in our family since 2012 with each sibling bringing their own unique story and experience to the cafe. We have been able to create a Decadent Shake bar away from the hustle and bustle of the busy shops and give our customers a place to call home.

The shakes we design and make have a lot of love in them, as friends and family work together to build these intriguing and deliciously decadent creations.

Growing up we were always competitive siblings. When we took over the family café in 2012 we started holding 'Thursday night experiments' where we would play around with tastes, textures, colors, shapes – anything you could think of. Apart from having a crazy amount of fun, these sessions were also where we founded some of our most decadent and delicious shake creations.

Whenever we create specials, it is Sarah and Matt that are all about the taste, while Brendan is always on top of aesthetic of the design. This has led to some of our craziest looking shakes, like the Double Decker, which includes a waffle AND a waffle cone – filled with mint chocolate and topped with caramels.

Or the Infamous Nutella Milkshake, which we created in 2013, and which was an instant hit, drawing chocolate fiends from every corner of the world to come and indulge in this unique, mind blowing shake.

The decadent shakes that you find in this book are the end result of beloved childhood memories, things that we as kids loved to indulge in (sometimes too much!).

Choosing just 40 shakes wasn't an easy task, but after countless hours sorting through the archives of our favorite concoctions, we landed on what you have before you, 40 of our most decadent creations, including the now famous (and infamous!) Nutella Milkshake, which continues to blow the minds and taste buds of everyone who dares to indulge.

There is something for every taste, even between the three of us we have really different tastes. Matt's favorite is the Salty Knickers – a mouth watering combination of pretzels and Snickersl Sarah raves about Billy Bonka – a insane combination of waffles, Snickers, Oreos, pretzels and peanut butter; and Brendan's a loyal sucker for Nutella, sour worms and Licorice, so the Infamous Nutella Milkshake is his go to.

We hope these shakes also serve as a source of inspiration for your own foodie creativity. They're a shining symbol of the importance of fun and not taking life too seriously. Have fun at home, go on a shopping frenzy and bring back an array of treats –sweet and savory – snacks, cake mix, candies, ice creams; you name it and just have a go!

Happy Shaking!

Notes about safety

Safety disclaimer: DO NOT attempt to eat off the chocolate or decorations that are melted onto the rim of the glass as the glass may crack when bitten.
If you must have the chocolate and decorations it is best to use a spoon to scrape off the melted chocolate.

With all milk based drinks, you can easily substitute milk for soy milk or any other products, however we do recommended adding 10 per cent more liquid, especially if you remove the ice cream, as the drink does not thicken up as much!

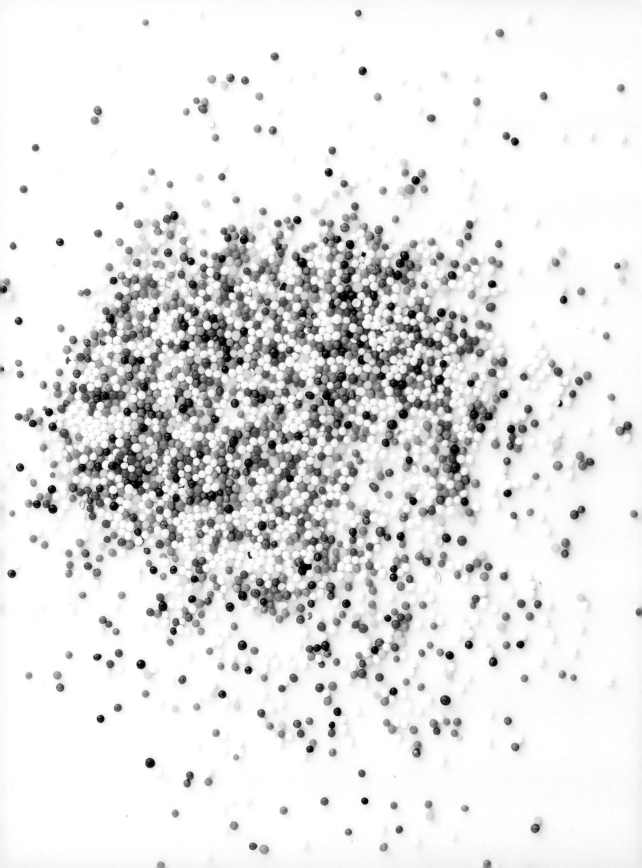

DECORATING YOUR GLASS

The effect of the chocolate rimmed glass is best achieved using bain marie of chocolate. Being home shake enthusiasts we don't expect you to have a bain marie to use, so you can grab Belgian milk chocolate and Belgian dark chocolate buds from your local supermarket and melt them in a pot on the stove. A good amount of chocolate for a chocolate rim is about 200g (7oz).

Chocolate Rim
Once the chocolate buds have been melted, dip the rim of the glass into the chocolate about 1cm (1/2 in) deep. Smoothly, roll the glass around so that all sides are covered. Place the glass in the fridge and let stand for at least 5 minutes.

Sugar Rim
The effect of the sugar rim is achieved by covering the rim of the glass with the juice of a slice of lemon or lime. Cover the rim with the juice 3–4 times and then quickly and evenly dip the rim of the glass into a cup of sugar and leave the glass to set in the fridge for a minimum of 20 minutes.

Whipped Cream
To add flavor, if you own a whipped cream cannister, add flavored syrups. At the cafe we use vanilla syrup for flavors (unless stated otherwise) however adding chocolate syrup turns the cream chocolate color or strawberry would turn the cream red. Keep this in mind if you want to crate your own Decadent Shakes for an added layer of color!

Extra Additions
To add sprinkles, coconut or anything other glass decorations, wait one minute after dipping the glass into the chocolate, and dip the glass into the sprinkles, coconut, or anything else you'd like to rim the glass and roll the glass around evenly coat the rim. Leave the glass in the fridge to set for a minimum of 30 minutes.

FRUITY MANIA

• Peach as Bro •

• Pash Me •

• Peachy Mango •

• Chainana •

• Man-Go-Crazy •

• Pina Colada •

• Mixed Berry Smoothie •

• Peach as Bro •

Shake ingredients:

375g (13oz) frozen peaches

8 frozen strawberries

200ml (7fl oz) passionfruit
 quencher

4 tsp strawberry syrup

4 tsp peach syrup

For presentation:

1 glass with sugar rim

1 long straw

1 lemon

1 mint sprig

125g (4oz) frozen mixed
 berries

Method:

» Place all the ingredients in a blender
 and mix until well combined. While
 the ingredients are blending, cut the
 lemon in half and start slicing into
 thin moon slices.

Decorate:

» Before pouring the mixture into the
 glass, create a sugar rim along the top
 of your glass (see page 13).

» Pour the blended mixture into the
 glass, until it reaches half way up to
 the rim.

» Place the straw on the inside right

hand side of the jar and place the 3
lemon slices on the left hand side of
straw, fanning them out as you slide
them in.

» Place the mint sprig in front of the
 straw and cover the remainder of the
 drink with frozen mixed berries.

» Serve immediately and enjoy!

» TIP: – The thinner the lemon slices,
 the better the drink looks when
 finished!

• Pash Me •

Shake ingredients:
handful fresh mint leaves
400ml (14fl oz) white
   peach and passionfruit
   quencher
handful of frozen fruits
   (mixed berries and peach)

For presentation:
1 glass with sugar rim
1 long straw
1 passionfruit (cut in half)
3 slices lemon
3 slices lime
ice cubes

- -

Method:

» Before pouring the mixture into the glass, create a sugar rim along the top of your glass (see page 13).

» Tear off 5 mint leaves and place them into the glass with the ice cubes.

» Place your lemon and lime slices and frozen fruit into the glass.

» Fill the glass to the rim with white peach and passionfruit quencher.

» Place a straw on the right side of the glass.

Decorate:

» Place half of the sliced passionfruit on top of the glass, bottom side up.

» Scoop the passionfruit pulp from the unused half onto the top of the drink to cover.

» Spread the remaining mint leaves around the passionfruit to create a flower.

» Serve immediately and enjoy!

» TIP: to make this quencher a frappe, just add ice and blend!

• Peachy Mango •

Shake ingredients:

7 cubes frozen mango

450g (15oz) diced frozen
   peaches

200ml (7fl oz) pineapple
   juice

2tbsp peach syrup

For presentation:

1 glass with sugar rim

1 long straw

250g (4oz) frozen mixed
   berries

1 lime, sliced

1 mint sprig

Method:

» Place all the ingredients in a blender
   jug and mix until well combined.
   While the ingredients are blending,
   slice the lime into thin slices.

Decorate:

» Before pouring the mixture into the
   glass, create a sugar rim along the top
   of your glass (see page 13).

» Pour the blended mixture into the
   glass until it reaches the rim.

» Place the straw on the right side of the
   glass and place three slices of lime on
   the left of the straw fanning out and
   away from the straw. Place the mint
   sprig in front of straw and use mixed
   berries to cover the top of the rest of
   the drink.

» Serve immediately and enjoy!

• Chainana •

Shake ingredients:
$^1/_2$ banana
3 scoops vanilla ice cream
200ml (7fl oz) milk
1 tsp honey
1 tbsp organic chai powder

For presentation:
1 chocolate rimmed glass
1 long straw
whipped cream
4 banana candies
1 cube Jersey Caramels

4 orange m&m's
1 cinnamon stick

Method:
- » Place all of the shake ingredients in a blender and mix until well combined.
- » While the ingredients are blending, slice up the Jersey Caramels into four pieces and tear the cinnamon stick into long thin pieces.

Decorate:
- » Before pouring the mixture into the glass, create a chocolate rim around the top of the glass (see page 13).
- » Pour in the blended mixture until it reaches halfway up the glass.
- » Place a straw in middle of the jar and fill the remainder of the jar with whipped cream.

- » Place the banana candies around the straw.
- » Slide the Jersey Caramels in between the banana candies and add one m&m in front of each jersey.
- » Sprinkle the cinnamon stick pieces around the straw.
- » Serve immediately and enjoy!

• Man-Go-Crazy •

Shake ingredients:

6 cubes frozen mango

2 mini Crunchie chocolate
  bars

250g (8oz) caramel popcorn

1 pump chocolate syrup

1 pump caramel syrup

2 scoops vanilla ice cream

200ml (7fl oz) milk

For presentation:

1 chocolate rimmed glass

1 long straw

1 waffle basket

2 scoops vanilla ice cream

melting chocolate

1 cinnamon donut

2 mini Crunchie chocolate
  bars

125g (4oz) caramel popcorn

1 syrup syringe

1 tsp caramel syrup

Method:

» Place all of the shake ingredients in a blender and mix until well combined.

» While the ingredients are blending, create a hole in the left/middle side of the waffle basket and crush the Crunchie into fine pieces.

Decorate:

» Before pouring the mixture into the glass, create a chocolate rim around the top of the glass (see page 13).

» Pour in the blended mixture until it reaches halfway up the glass.

» Place a straw through the hole in the waffle basket and place 2 scoops of ice cream into the basket.

» Melt the melting chocolate as per the directions on the packet. Dip one side of the donut into the melted chocolate and then dip the donut into the crushed up Crunchie.

» Once the donut has dried, place it over the straw.

» Scatter the caramel popcorn on top of the ice cream.

» Fill syringe with caramel syrup and place on right side of donut.

» Drizzle the remaining melted chocolate and crushed Crunchie over the caramel popcorn.

» Serve immediately and enjoy!

• Pina Colada •

Ingredients:

125g (4oz) diced frozen
    pineapple pieces
200ml (7fl oz) pineapple
    juice
5 ice cubes

1 ¹/₂ heaped tbsp shredded
    coconut

For Presentation:
1 chocolate rimmed glass
1 long straw

brown sugar
shredded coconut
1 kiwi fruit, sliced
1 stem fresh mint
2 yellow Jubes
1 mini chocolate flake bar

Method:

» Place all the shake ingredients in a blender and mix until well combined. While the ingredients are spinning, slice the kiwi into thin slices.

Decorate:

» Before pouring the mixture into the glass, create a chocolate rim around the top of the glass (see page 13).

» Pour the ingredients into the glass until it reaches the rim.

» Place the straw at the back of the glass leaning towards the right and fill the rest of the glass with shredded coconut. Place the stem of mint in the glass on the left side of straw.

» Place the sliced kiwi fruit slightly in front of the straw, so that it covers the mint.

» Add in the yellow Jubes, placing them in front of the mint.

» Finish the drink by breaking up the flake chocolate bar and sprinkling it over the drink.

» Serve immediately and enjoy!

• Mixed Berry Smoothie •

Shake ingredients:

125g (4oz) frozen mixed
   berries
3 scoops vanilla ice cream
200ml (7fl oz) milk
1 teaspoon strawberry
   syrup

For presentation:

1 chocolate rimmed glass
1 long straw
handful desiccated coconut
1 stem of fresh mint leaves
red and purple mini jelly
   lollies
2 jelly mint leaves

2 chocolate Pocky Sticks
1 small waffle cone, with
   chocolate and coconut
   rim.

Method:

» Place all the shake ingredients in a blender and mix until well combined.

» Before pouring the mixture into the glass, create a chocolate rim around the top of the glass (see page 13).

» Once the chocolate rim is almost dry, layer on the desiccated coconut around the rim.

» Pour the ingredients into the glass until it reaches the rim.

» Cover the top of the mixture with the remaining desiccated coconut.

» Cut a hole in the base of the waffle cone and place the cone at the back of the glass.

» Weave the straw through the cone and into the shake.

» Remove the mint leaves from the stem and place the leaves in the waffle cone.

» Place the red and purple mini jelly lollies around the rim of the glass, alternating in color.

» Place the 2 jelly mint leaves in front of the waffle cone.

» Place the two chocolate Pocky Sticks at the back of the cone.

» Serve immediately and enjoy!

CHOCOLATE MANIA

• Crunchie Kisses •

• Chocolate Milkshake •

• Malt my Heart •

• Mocha Madness •

• Salty Knickers •

• Magic Doodle •

• Double Decker •

• Mc'Mazing •

• Iced Chocolate •

• Bueno Mars •

• Jenga •

• Twerk it •

• Coachella •

• Billy Bonka •

• Crunchie Kisses •

Shake ingredients:
2 small Crunchie chocolate
    bars
3 fresh strawberries
1 Kinder Bueno stick
200ml (7fl oz) milk
1 tbsp vanilla custard
1 Kinder egg
7 ice cubes

For presentation:
1 chocolate covered glass
1 long straw
half cinnamon donut
Persian fairy floss
2 Pocky Sticks
1 mini Crunchie chocolate
    bars
2 small red jelly frogs

4 Ovaltines
sprinkles
1 Kinder chocolate stick
$^1/_2$ Kinder Bueno chocolate
    stick
whipped cream, to fill
sprinkles

Method:

» Place all of the shake ingredients into a blender and mix until well combined.

Decorate:

» Before pouring the mixture into the glass, create a chocolate rim around the top of the glass (see page 13).

» Pour the blended mixture into the glass until it reaches the rim.

» Place the straw at the back in the middle of glass. Fill the remainder of the jar with whipped cream.

» Place the half cinnamon donut in front of the straw to the left side of the glass, hooking it over the side of the glass.

» Place 2 red jelly frogs in front of the donut so that the frogs are on the edge of the glass.

» Place 3 Pocky Sticks on the right hand side of straw and place the Kinder stick and Kinder Bueno in front of the Pocky Sticks.

» Cut the small Crunchie in half and place both halves on the right hand side of the glass.

» Put a small amount of whipped cream on top of the donut and then top with the Persian fairy floss.

» Top the fairy floss with a sprinkling of Ovaltines and sprinkles.

» Serve immediately and enjoy!

• Chocolate Milkshake •

Shake ingredients:
3 pumps chocolate syrup
2 scoops vanilla ice cream
300ml (10fl oz) milk

For presentation:
1 chocolate rimmed glass
1 long straw
1 jelly snake

Rice Bubbles
colored popcorn

. . . .

Method:
» Place all ingredients in a blender and mix until well combined.

Decorate:
» Before pouring the mixture into the glass, create a chocolate rim around the top of the glass (see page 13).
» Pour the blended mixture into the glass until it reaches the rim of the glass.
» Scatter the Rice Bubbles over the shake until it is entirely covered.
» Place a straw on right side of milkshake.
» Wrap a jelly snake around the straw and place colored popcorn on top of the Rice Bubbles until the glass is completely covered.

» TIP: Repeat this recipe for other classic milkshake flavors such like slimy lime, super strawberry, nana banana, crazy caramel and very cool vanilla.

• Malt my Heart •

Shake ingredients:
1 ¹/₂ tbsp malt
3 pumps chocolate syrup
2 scoops vanilla ice cream
200ml (7fl oz) milk
2 mini chocolate Flake bars

For presentation:
1 chocolate rimmed glass
1 long straw
3 Maltesers chocolate
8 m&m's
whipped cream

1 chocolate Flake bar, crushed

Method:
» Place all the ingredients into a blender and mix until well combined.
» While milkshake is blending, chop up the Maltesers into halves and set aside for decorating. Crush up the chocolate flake bar and set aside.

Decorate:
» Before pouring the mixture into the glass, create a chocolate rim around the top of the glass (see page 13).
» Pour the blended mixture into the glass until it reaches the rim.
»   Place the Maltesers around the edge of the jar leaving a small gap in between.

» Place the m&m's in between the Maltesers and cover them with whipped cream with the crushed chocolate Flake pieces.
» Serve immediately and enjoy!

• Mocha Madness •

Shake ingredients:

1 tsp coffee
3 pumps chocolate syrup
2 scoops vanilla ice cream
250ml (8fl oz) milk

For presentation:

1 chocolate rimmed glass
1 long straw
whipped cream
125g (4oz) mixed m&m's
1 chocolate Flake bar

Method:

» Place all the ingredients in a blender and mix until well combined.
» While the ingredients are mixing, crush up the flake and add to your chocolate rimmed glass at set aside.

» Place straw in the middle and fill the remainder with whipped cream.
» Cover the cream in the m&m's.
» Serve immediately and enjoy!

Decorate:

» Before pouring the mixture into the glass, create a chocolate rim around the top of the glass (see page 13).
» Pour the blended mixture into the glass until it reaches the bottom of the rim.

• Salty Knickers •

Shake ingredients:

250g (8oz) salty pretzels

4 mini Snickers bars

1 tbsp smooth peanut butter

2 pumps caramel syrup

1 pump chocolate syrup

2 scoops vanilla ice cream

200ml (7fl oz) milk

For presentation:

1 chocolate rimmed glass

1 long straw

whipped cream

chocolate powder, to sprinkle

2 salty pretzels

1 mini Snickers bars

60g (2oz) peanut granules

- -

Method:

» Place all the ingredients in a blender and mix until well combined.

» While the mixture is blending, slice the Snickers bars and set aside for decorating.

Decorate:

» Before pouring the mixture into the glass, create a chocolate rim around the top of the glass (see page 13).

» Pour in the blended mixture until it reaches the bottom of the rim.

» Place a straw in the middle, back of the glass and create a mini tower with whipped cream.

» Dust chocolate powder over the whipped cream and place two pretzels upside down in front of straw. Place two pieces of the sliced Snickers bar in front of one pretzel, and two in front of the other pretzel.

» Sprinkle peanut granules over the shake to serve.

» Serve immediately and enjoy!

• Magic Doodle •

Shake ingredients:
2 mini Crunchie bars
3 Oreo biscuits
1 tbsp Nutella
1 tsp caramel syrup
8 ice cubes
100ml (3fl oz) milk

For presentation:
1 chocolate rimmed glass
1 long straw
1 Oreo cookie
3 Pokey sticks
1 small packet of Mammy
  noodles

handful of mini m&m's
2 mini red frogs

Method:

» Place all the ingredients in a blender and mix until well combined.

» While the mixture is blending, slice the Snickers bars and set aside for decorating.

Decorate:

» Before pouring the mixture into the glass, create a chocolate rim around the top of the glass (see page 13).

» Pour in the blended mixture until it reaches the bottom of the rim.

» Place a straw in the middle, back of the glass and create a mini tower with whipped cream.

» Place the Pokey sticks at the back of the glass to the right of the straw.

» Break up the Mammy noodles lengthways and place three strips of noodles in front of the straw.

» Place the red frogs on the edge of the jar, in front of the noodles and then cover the remaining cream with mini m&m's to serve.

» Serve immediately and enjoy!

• Double Decker •

Shake ingredients:

1 mint Golden Gaytime ice cream

2 mini Crunchie chocolate bars

1 tbsp Nutella

1 pump caramel syrup

1 pump chocolate syrup

2 scoops vanilla ice cream

200ml (7fl oz) milk

For presentation:

1 chocolate rimmed glass

1 long straw

drizzle chocolate syrup

1 large waffle cone

melting chocolate

1 scoop vanilla ice cream

whipped cream

1 waffle basket

half block mint chocolate

5 chocolate chips

2 toffees

1 mini Crunchie chocolate bars, chopped

chocolate krispy balls

chocolate whipped cream

5 skinless roasted hazelnuts

. . . .

Method:

» Place all the ingredients in a blender and mix until well combined.

» While the mixture is blending, melt the melting chocolate and create a hole in the base of the waffle cone. Dip the cone into the melting chocolate and set aside to cool

» Create the chocolate whipped cream by mixing together chocolate syrup with the whipped cream.

Decorate:

» Before pouring the mixture into the glass, create a chocolate rim around the top of the glass (see page 13).

» Pour in the blended mixture until it reaches the bottom of the rim.

» Place the waffle cone on top of glass and place a straw on a diagonal leaning left.

» Place scoop of ice cream in the cone in front of the straw and fill the waffle cone with whipped cream.

» Sit the cone through the straw leaning left and fill cone half way with whipped cream, then crumble mint chocolate over the cream until the cone is filled until the top.

» Staring from the right side of basket cone, create a wave of chocolate chips in direction towards the front of the basket.

» Place one hazelnut in front of each chocolate chip and place the chopped up Crunchie pieces in front of the cone.

» At the front of the waffle basket place two toffees and cover the rest of the whipped cream with chocolate krispy balls.

• Mc'Mazing •

Shake ingredients

4 Oreo cookies

250g (8oz) mini m&m's

3 scoops vanilla ice cream

200ml (7fl oz) milk

For presentation:

1 piccolo glass

melting chocolate

1 long straw

1 scoop cone

sprinkles

1 long dessert spoon

1 jelly snake

2 chocolate Pocky Sticks

2 large Oreo cookies

1 mini ice cream cone

1 scoop ice cream

mini m&m's

3 Crispy m&m's

2 mini Oreo cookies

1 tsp caramel syrup

1 syrup syringe

1 board

- -

Method:

» Place all the ingredients in a blender and mix until well combined.

» While the ingredients are mixing, melt the chocolate and dip your piccolo glass and cone into the chocolate. Also dip your cone into sprinkles before placing both in the fridge to set.

Decorate:

» Once set, fill the glass with the blended mixture until it reaches the bottom of the rim.

» Place a straw and long spoon towards the back of the glass and tie them together using a jelly snake. Give two pumps of caramel syrup to the piccolo glass and then fill the glass with mini m&m's.

» Place two Pokey Sticks in the piccolo glass at the back middle.

» Place half biscuit at the front, right of the glass. Place the ice cream cone on the right side of the piccolo glass.

» Place the ice cream on top of cone and decorate the ice cream with crispy m's and mini Oreos.

» Fill the syrup syringe with caramel syrup and place syringe in front of piccolo and cone.

» Serve immediately and enjoy!

• Iced Chocolate •

Shake ingredients:

3 pumps chocolate syrup
1 scoop ice cream
300ml (10fl oz) milk

For presentation:

1 chocolate dipped and
  sprinkle covered glass
1 long straw
4 different candies of your

choosing
whipped cream
sprinkles

Method:

» Before pouring the mixture into the
  glass, create a chocolate rim around
  the top of the glass and top with
  sprinkles (see page 13).

» Pump three squirts of chocolate syrup
  around the inside of the glass.

» Place 1 scoop of ice cream neatly into
  the bottom of the glass and fill the
  glass up with milk until it reaches the
  rim.

» Fill remainder with whipped cream
  tower to about 4–6cm (1.5–2in) high.

Decorate:

» Create your masterpiece! Have fun
  making nice patterns with the candies
  of your choice and create a unique
  iced chocolate.

» Serve immediately and enjoy!

» Tip: If you're not a fan of the iced
  chocolate, you can use caramel or
  strawberry syrup instead!

• Bueno Mars •

Shake ingredients:
3 Kinder Bueno bar stick
2 mini Mars Bars
7 frozen raspberries
$1/4$ banana
2 scoops vanilla ice cream
200ml (7fl oz)milk

For presentation:
1 chocolate rimmed glass
whipped cream
1 long straw
whipped cream
1 Kinder Bueno stick
1 mint sprig

1 mini Mars Bar
2 skinless hazelnuts
5 frozen raspberries
icing sugar, sifted

. . . .

Method:
» Place all ingredients in blender and mix until well combined.

Decorate:
» Before pouring the mixture into the glass, create a chocolate rim around the top of the glass (see page 13).
» Pour in the blended mixture until it reaches the base of the glass rim.
» Place a straw at the back, middle of the glass.
» Fill the remaining space in the glass with whipped cream.
» Chop the Kinder Bueno stick in half and place both halves on right hand side of the glass.

» Place the mint sprig on the left side of the straw, making sure that only the leaves are seen.
» Place the mini Mars Bar in front of the mint sprig and place one hazelnut on each side of the Mars Bar. Cover what is left of the whipped cream with frozen raspberries and sprinkle with icing sugar.
» Serve immediately and enjoy!

• Jenga •

Shake ingredients:

3 Oreo cookies

2 white Tim Tams (or
   white chocolate cookies)

1 tbsp Nutella

$1/2$ tbsp peanut butter

2 scoops vanilla ice cream

200ml (7fl oz) milk

For presentation:

1 long straw

whipped cream

2 Cookies and Cream Kit
   Kat, broken into sticks (or
   any cookies and cream
   flavored chocolate bars)

1 mint sprig

Method:

» Place all of the shake ingredients in a
   blender and mix until well combined.

Decorate:

» Place a straw in the middle of the
   glass and fill the remaining space with
   whipped cream.

» Place two Kit Kat sticks horizontally
   on edge of jar. Place the next two Kit
   Kat sticks horizontally the opposite
   way.

» Repeat the Kit Kat stack two more
   times, then place the mint sprig in the
   middle in front of the straw and there
   you have it, your very own Jenga to
   drink!

» Serve immediately and enjoy!

• Twerk it •

Ingredients:
125g (4oz) ice cubes
125ml (4fl oz) milk
3 mini Twix sticks
3 tbsp caramel syrup
pinch of salt
1 tsp malt

For presentation:
1 chocolate covered glass
1 long straw
whipped cream
4 original salt flavor
    crinkle crisps
1 cube caramel fudge

4 orange Smarties
1 stem of mint leaves

Method:
»   Place all of the shake ingredients into a blender and mix until well combined.

Decorate:
»   Before pouring the mixture into the glass, create a chocolate rim around the top of the glass (see page 13).
»   Pour the blended mixture into the glass until it reaches the rim and then fill the remaining space with whipped cream.
»   Place straw in the class towards the back left.
»   Create a fan using the crisps at the back, right of the straw.

»   Chop Twix bar in half and place both pieces on the left, outside of the straw
»   Place the mint leaves in front of the straw, between the crisps and the Twix.
»   Slice the caramel fudge cube and place three small pieces in front of the chips.
»   Cover the remaining space with orange Smarties.
»   Serve immediately and enjoy!

• Coachella •

Shake ingredients:

1 tbsp Nutella

1 ½ tbsp coconut oil

5 lychees (fresh is best
  otherwise your local
  supermarket should have
  tinned)

3 scoops vanilla ice cream

200ml milk (7oz)

For presentation:

1 chocolate rimmed glass

1 long straw

melting chocolate

8 skinless roasted
  hazelnuts

2 Maltesers

coconut chips

1 mini waffle cone

desiccated coconut

fresh mint

whipped cream

Method:

» Place all of the shake ingredients in a
  blender and mix until well combined.

» While the ingredients are blending,
  cut 2cm (1in) off the cone, and dip
  the cone in melted chocolate and
  desiccated coconut. Leave aside to set.

Decorate:

» Before pouring the mixture into the
  glass, create a chocolate rim around
  the top of the glass (see page 13).

» Pour in the blended mixture until it
  reaches the bottom of the rim of the
  glass.

» Place a straw in the back, middle of
  the glass and fill with the remaining

space with whipped cream. Place the
cone over the straw, sliding the straw
through the hole in the cone.

» Fill the cone with fresh mint leaves.

» Place hazelnuts on the edge of the
  front of the glass and cone and cover
  the cream with coconut chips.

» Finish off by placing two Maltesers in
  front of cone, on top of the coconut
  chips.

» Serve immediately and enjoy!

• Billy Bonka •

Shake ingredients:
3 Oreo cookies
2 mini Snickers bar
1 tbsp peanut butter
2 pumps chocolate syrup
3 scoops vanilla ice cream
200ml (6fl oz) milk

For presentation:
2 mini waffles
1 chocolate rimmed glass
1 long straw
7 large twisted pretzels
2 large Oreo cookies
4 mini Oreo cookies

Whipped cream
handful Reeces pieces

Method:

» Place all of the shake ingredients in a blender and mix until well combined.

Decorate:

» Before pouring the mixture into the glass, create a chocolate rim around the top of the glass (see page 13).
» Pour in the blended mixture until it reaches the bottom of the rim of the glass and fill the remainder of the glass with whipped cream.
» Poke holes through two mini waffles and layer one on top of the glass.
» Cover the waffle with whipped cream, and two opened large Oreo biscuits.
» Top the Oreos with 4 pretzels and a sprinkling of Reeces Pieces.

» Layer on the second mini waffle and top with whipped cream.
» Top the cream with opened mini Oreo cookies and the remaining pretzels.
» Sprinkle with Reeces Pieces.
» Serve immediately and enjoy.

SUPER SWEET

• Vivo la Vogue •

• Brittany's Musketeers •

• The Hike •

• Maybe it's Maple •

• Fairies Dream •

• Hubba Hubba •

• Bang Bang Meringue •

• Creaming Soda Spider •

• Pink Lady •

• Vivo la Vogue •

Shake ingredients:

1 packet creaming soda
  jelly
3 Iced VoVo biscuits
1 tsp strawberry jam (jelly)
4 marshmallows
30ml (1fl oz) vanilla
  custard

3 scoops vanilla ice cream
200ml (7fl oz) milk

For presentation:

1 chocolate rimmed glass
1 long straw
1 ½ Iced VoVo
whipped cream

5 mini pink marshmallows
5 mini white
  marshmallows
1 tsp strawberry jam
1 tsp shredded coconut
1 red jelly frog

Method:

» The day before, prepare the creaming soda jelly as per the instructions on the packet. For best results, once the mixture is made, pour 30ml (1fl oz) of the jelly into a chocolate rimmed glass (see page 13) and leave it in the fridge to set overnight.

» The next day, place all of the shake ingredients into a blender and mix until well combined.

» While the shake is blending, cut the Iced VoVo biscuits in to thirds.

Decorate:

» Pour the blended mixture into the jelly filled glass and place a straw at middle, back of the glass.

» Fill the remaining space with whipped cream.

» Place the Iced VoVo pieces on top of the cream on the front and right side of the straw.

» Place mini marshmallows, alternating between white and pink, around the rim of the glass.

» Place the strawberry jam in middle of the shake to cover whipped cream.

» Sprinkle the jam with shredded coconut and top with a red jelly frog.

» Serve immediately and enjoy!

• Brittany's Musketeers •

Shake ingredients:

3 musk sticks

4 sherbet balls

125g (4oz) fairy floss

3 scoops lolly bag flavored
   ice cream

200ml (7fl oz) milk

For presentation:

1 chocolate rimmed glass

1 long straw

whipped cream

1 sherbet lollypop

4 sherbet sticks

fairy floss

6 pink musk sticks

sprinkles

Method:

» Place all the ingredients in a blender
   and mix until well combined.

Decorate:

» Before pouring the mixture into the
   glass, create a chocolate rim around
   the top of the glass (see page 13).

» Pour in the blended mixture until it
   reaches halfway the bottom of the
   rim.

» Place a straw on the right side of the
   shake and fill the remaining space
   with whipped cream.

» Place a sherbet lollypop inside the
   straw and place four sherbet sticks to
   the right of the straw.

» Create a tower with the fairy floss,
   and create a tower with the musk
   sticks on top of the shake.

» Serve immediately and enjoy!

• Pink Lady •

Shake ingredients:
5 strawberries
3 scoops ice cream
2 tbsp maple syrup
200ml (5fl oz) milk
2 teaspoon strawberry
    syrup

For presentation:
1 chocolate rimmed glass
1 long straw
1 cinnamon donut
1 pikelet
1 small syrup syringe
2 tsp maple syrup
Pink whipped cream

8 strawberries and cream
    candies
1 stem fresh mint
small handful dessicated
    coconut
Icing sugar, sifted

Method:
» Place all the ingredients in a blender
  and mix until well combined.

Decorate:
» Before pouring the mixture into the
  glass, create a chocolate rim around
  the top of the glass and coat with
  dessicated coconut (see page 13).
» Pour in the blended mixture until it
  reaches the bottom of the rim.
» Place straw at the back, left of the
  glass.
» Place the donut on the rim of jar, layer
  the pikelet on top and cover the top of
  the pikelet with whipped cream.
» Fill the syrup syringe with maple
  syrup and place the syringe in the

middle of the glass poking into the
pikelet.
» Top the pikelet with mint leaves.
» Place the strawberries and cream
  candies on the rim of the cream
  creating on top.
» Sprinkle the glass with icing sugar.
» Serve immediately and enjoy!

• The Hike •

Shake ingredients:

1 pikelet

$^1/_2$ banana

2 ginger kisses

1 tbsp maple syrup

1 tsp organic chai

1 tsp honey

2 scoops ice vanilla ice

cream

200ml (7fl oz) milk

For presentation:

1 chocolate rimmed glass

1 long straw

1 pikelet

Nutella

4 round slices fresh
banana

1 mini chocolate flake,
crushed

handful chocolate krispy
balls

- -

Method:

» Place all the ingredients in a blender and mix until well combined.

» While the ingredients are blending spread Nutella liberally over the pikelet.

Decorate:

» Before pouring the mixture into the glass, create a chocolate rim around the top of the glass (see page 13).

» Pour in the blended mixture until it reaches the bottom of the rim.

» Place the pikelet over the straw, pushing the straw through the pikelet

until the pikelet is sitting flap on top of the glass.

» Place the sliced banana around the straw and sprinkle generously with the crushed chocolate flake. Sprinkle with chocolate krispy balls to finish.

» Serve immediately and enjoy!

• Maybe it's Maple •

Shake ingredients:
2 tsp maple syrup
3 scoops vanilla ice cream
1 tsp caramel syrup
60g (2 oz) pecan
100ml (3fl oz) milk

For presentation:
1 chocolate rimmed glass
1 long straw
125g (4 oz) pecans
7 edible dried roses
1 small pecan pie
handful chocolate Persian
  fairy floss

Crispy chocolate balls
Icing sugar, to sprinkle
1 small empty pie shell

· ·

Method:
»   Place all the ingredients in a blender
    and mix until well combined.

Decorate:
»   Before pouring the mixture into the
    glass, create a chocolate rim around
    the top of the glass (see page 13).
»   Pour in the blended mixture until it
    reaches the bottom of the rim, and
    fill the remainder of the glass with
    whipped cream.
»   Place the straw in the back middle of
    the glass.
»   Place 4 pecans on the edge of the glass
    towards the front, placing edible dried

roses in between.
»   Sprinkle with crispy chocolate balls.
»   Place the pecan pie on top of the
    whipped cream and poke a hole
    through the pie into the glass.
»   Place 3 pecans on top of the pie and
    top with chocolate Persian fairy floss
    and crispy chocolate balls.
»   Cut a hole in the base of the pie smell
    and place it on top of the glass.
»   Fill the pie shell with chocolate
    Persian fairy floss, edible dried roses
    and crispy chocolate balls.
»   Dust with icing sugar.
»   Serve immediately and enjoy!

• Fairies Dream •

Shake ingredients:
4 large Oreo cookies
60g (2oz) pink fairy floss
125g (4oz) sprinkles
1 tsp peach syrup
2 scoops vanilla ice cream

200ml (7fl oz) milk

For presentation:
1 chocolate rimmed glass
1 long straw
whipped cream

1 slice white bread
  buttered
sprinkles
1 musk stick
1 large Oreo cookie
1 mini Oreo cookie

Method:
» Place all ingredients in a blender and mix until well combined.
» While the shake is mixing butter the bread, cover with sprinkles and cut into triangular slices.

Decorate:
» Before pouring the mixture into the glass, create a chocolate rim around the top of the glass (see page 13).
» Pour in the blended mixture until it reaches the base of the glass rim.
» Place your straw to the left and cover the remaining space with whipped cream.
» From the back of the jar, place one slice of bread in front of the other making sure the tip of the triangle is facing to the right.
» Separate the large Oreo and place the cream side of the cookie on left piece of bread with the other piece slightly in front.
» Separate the mini Oreo and place both chocolate sides one in front of each large Oreo.
» Place the musk stick in the middle of the bread, just behind the two large Oreo cookies and the fairy dream is complete.
» Serve immediately and enjoy!

• Hubba Hubba •

Shake ingredients:
1 lime Splice ice cream
60g (2oz) mixed berries
2 pumps lime syrup
2 scoops vanilla ice cream
200ml (7 fl oz) milk

For presentation:
1 chocolate rimmed glass
1 long straw
2 pieces grapefruit
  chewing gum
2 Froot Loop rings
2 Jubes

1 candy banana
1 small kebab skewer
whipped cream
7 gumballs
Wonka Nerds

Method:
» Place all the ingredients in a blender and mix until well combined.
» While the ingredients are mixing, layer the candy banana, 2 Froot Loop rings, 1 piece of grapefruit chewing gum (wrapped removed) and Jube onto a small kebab skewer.

Decorate:
» Before pouring the mixture into the glass, create a chocolate rim around the top of the glass (see page 13).
» Pour in the blended mixture until it reaches the bottom of the rim.
» Place straw at the back, left of the glass and fill the remaining space with whipped cream.
» Place one piece of grape fruit chewing gum (wrapper on) in front of straw in a diagonal.
» Place your candy skewer on the right side of straw and create a rim at front of shake with the gumballs. Cover the remaining whipped cream with Nerds.
» Serve immediately and enjoy!

• Bang Bang Meringue •

Shake ingredients:

30ml (1fl oz) passionfruit
    pulp
5 frozen strawberries
1 tsp honey
200ml (7fl oz) traditional
    lemonade
4 meringue drops
6 ice cubes

For presentation:

1 glass with sugar rim
1 long straw
1 meringue nest
1 sherbet stick
3 strawberry clouds
    candies
3 pink m&m candies
Persian fairy floss

1 sour strawberry strip
1 sour bubblegum strip
sprinkles

Method to make:

» Place all the shake ingredients in a
blender and mix until well combined.

Decorate:

» Before pouring the mixture into the
glass, create a sugar rim around the
top of the glass (see page 13).
» Pour the blended mixture into the
glass until it reaches the rim.
» Place the meringue nest on top of the
drink and use the straw to create a
hole in the meringue nest.
» Place the strawberry clouds on the
right hand side of the straw.
» Chop the sherbet stick into 3 pieces

and place each piece on the right side
of the strawberry clouds. Place of the
Persian fairy floss in middle, then
place 3 pink m&m candies on left
side of the fairy floss. Wrap the sour
strawberry strip around the straw
and then use the sour bubblegum
strip to tie a knot to hold together the
strawberry sour strap and the straw.
» Finish off by adding sprinkles over the
top of the drink.
» Serve immediately and enjoy!

• Creaming Soda Spider •

Ingredients:

1 sugar rimmed glass
1 long straw
strawberry syrup
1 scoop vanilla ice cream

1 can creaming soda
2 red jelly snake
3 strawberries and cream
  jelly candies
2 red jelly frogs

2 red Gummi Bears
sprinkles

Method:

» Before pouring the mixture into the glass, create a sugar rim around the top of the glass (see page 13).

» Pour the strawberry syrup around the inside of the glass (the more you use, the stronger the taste!).

» Place a scoop of ice cream into the bottom and then throw in all of the candies.

» Finish with a topping of sprinkles.

» Finish with sprinkles.

» Pour in the creaming soda.

» Serve with a spoon and a straw.

» Serve immediately and enjoy!

CRAZY COOL

• Infamous Nutella Milkshake •

• Custarted •

• Infamous Peanut Butter Milkshake •

• Wheel of Fortune •

• Fifi's Fairy Tale •

• TVC Tree •

• My Kind of Kool •

• Terry and Sue •

• Infamous Nutella Milkshake •

Shake ingredients:

1 scoop vanilla ice cream

3 tsp Nutella

1 pump chocolate syrup

200ml (7fl oz) milk

For presentation:

1 chocolate rimmed glass

1 long straw

whipped cream

7 sour worms

7 hazelnuts (skinless and
  roasted)

½ licorice all sorts

1 mini wafer cone

2 pieces of colored popcorn

dusting chocolate powder

whipped cream (to fill ¼ jar)

- -

Method:

» Place all the ingredients into a blender and mix until well combined.

» While the ingredients are blending, cut the end of the wafer cone and dip it into melted chocolate then sprinkles.

Decorate:

» Before pouring the mixture into the glass, create a chocolate rim around the top of the glass (see page 13).

» Pour the blended mixture into the glass until it is about 2cm (1in) away from the rim.

» Place a straw at the back of the glass and fill the remaining space with whipped cream.

» Place the cut and chocolate dipped cone over the straw.

» Scatter the hazelnuts around the rim of the glass.

» Place the sliced licorice pieces in front of the cone.

» Place the colored popcorn inside the cone and then fill cone with sour worms.

» Sprinkle the finished drink with chocolate powder to just lightly cover the decoration.

» Serve immediately and enjoy!

• Custarted •

Ingredients:

5 cubes mango
60ml (2fl oz) vanilla
    custard
5 chocolate Tim Tams
2 tbsp Milo
1 tbsp organic cocoa oil
2 scoops vanilla ice cream
200ml (7fl oz) milk

For presentation:

1 chocolate sprinkle dipped
    glass
1 long straw
sprinkles
1 waffle basket
2 scoops vanilla ice cream
whipped cream
1 mini chocolate waffle

yellow Persian fairy floss
3 mini chocolate Tim Tams
1 tbsp Milo
60g (2oz) chocolate krispy
    balls
1 Tim Tam, crushed
melting chocolate
1 mini meringue nest

Method:

» Place all the ingredients in a blender jug, and mix until well combined.

» While the ingredients are blending, heat up the melting chocolate and cut a hole in the waffle basket.

» Dip your waffle and the tip of the meringue nest into melted chocolate and then into the sprinkles. Leave both aside to set.

Decorate:

» Before pouring the mixture into the glass, create a chocolate rim around the top of the glass and roll the glass in sprinkles (see page 13).

» Pour in the blended mixture until it reaches the bottom of the rim.

» Place the waffle basket on top of the glass and slide the straw through the hole.

» Put two scoops of ice cream in front of the straw and fill the remainder of the waffle basket with whipped cream.

» Slide the chocolate waffle through the straw and then place a layer of fairy floss on top of the chocolate waffle.

» Spike your meringue through the straw and place three mini Tim Tams at the front of the waffle basket.

» Cover the remainder of the shake with whipped cream, sprinkles, Milo, chocolate krispy balls and crushed up Tim Tam to finish.

» Serve immediately and enjoy!

• Infamous Peanut Butter Milkshake •

Ingredients:

3 tsp smooth peanut butter

1 pump caramel syrup

1 pump chocolate syrup

1 scoop vanilla ice cream

200ml (7fl oz) milk

For presentation:

1 mini cone

6 sour coke bottles

15 peanut bite Reeses
  Pieces

1 colored popcorn

dusting of chocolate
  powder

whipped cream (to fill $^1/_4$
  jar)

. . . .

Method:

» Place all ingredients in a blender and mix until well combined.

» While the ingredients are mixing cut the bottom off the mini cone, dip it in chocolate and sprinkles and set aside.

Decorate:

» Before pouring the mixture into the glass, create a chocolate rim around the top of the glass (see page 13)

» Pour the blended mixture into the glass until it reaches the bottom of the rim.

» Place a straw in the shake, towards the back of the glass.

» Place straw at the back of the jar.

» Fill the rest of the jar with whipped cream.

» Place the cone on the straw topside up, and fill the cone with colored popcorn.

» Cover the whipped cream with Reese's Pieces.

» Place the sour coke bottles inside the cone and finish with a small dusting of chocolate powder.

» Serve immediately and enjoy!

• Wheel of Fortune •

Shake ingredients:
1 large Wagon Wheel
6 large marshmallows
2 tbsp strawberry jam
1 tbsp peanut butter
3 scoops vanilla ice cream

200ml (7fl oz) milk

For presentation:
1 chocolate rimmed glass
1 long straw
whipped cream

1 small Wagon Wheel
6 white mini
    marshmallows
chocolate krispy balls
1 mini chocolate Flake bar,
    crushed

Method:
» Place all the ingredients in a blender and mix until well combined.
» While the ingredients are blending, slice the small Wagon Wheel into quarters and set aside.

Decorate:
» Before pouring the mixture into the glass, create a chocolate rim around the top of the glass (see page 13).
» Pour in the blended mixture until it reaches the bottom of the rim. Fill the remainder of the jar with whipped cream.
» Place your Wagon Wheel quarters on the right side of glass creating a fan.
» On the left side of the glass, scatter the mini marshmallows and chocolate krispy balls.
» Sprinkle the crushed chocolate Flake bar over the shake to finish.
» Serve immediately and enjoy!

• Fifi's Fairy Tale •

Shake ingredients:

3 mini Crunchie chocolate
  bars
2 tbsp caramel fudge
2 chocolate chip cookies
pinch of salt

For presentation:

1 chocolate rimmed glass
1 long straw
1 cinnamon donut
whipped cream
small handful of white

Persian fairy floss
1 Pocky stick, green tea
  flavored
fresh flowers (your choice)
dried rose petals

Method:

» Place all the ingredients in a blender
  and mix until well combined.

Decorate:

» Before pouring the mixture into the
  glass, create a chocolate rim around
  the top of the glass (see page 13).
» Pour in the blended mixture until it
  reaches halfway the bottom of the
  rim.
» Place the cinnamon donut on top of
  the glass and put the straw through
  the middle of the donut, into the
  shake.

» Cover donut with whipped cream and
  white Persian fairy floss.
» Place the Pocky stick on left side of
  straw and layer the glass with fresh
  flowers.
» Sprinkle the shake with dried rose
  petals.
» Serve immediately and enjoy!

• TVC Tree •

Shake ingredients:
4 brownie flavored Mars
   Bars
2 Oreo cookies
1 tbsp malt
25ml vanilla custard (0.8oz)
7 ice cubes
1 tbsp Nutella

200ml (7fl oz) milk

For presentation:
1 chocolate rimmed glass
1 long straw
whipped cream
green die
3 chocolate gold coins

1 mini waffle cone
gold tinsel
red crispy m&ms
Maltesers
chocolate star
icing sugar, sifted

Method:
» Place all the ingredients in a blender and mix until well combined.
» While the ingredients are blending, mix together the whipped cream with green food dye.

Decorate:
» Before pouring the mixture into the glass, create a chocolate rim around the top of the glass (see page 13).
» Pour in the blended mixture until it reaches the bottom of the rim.

» Fill rest of glass with plain whipped cream and place the three gold coins around the glass.
» Place the mini cone upside down on top of the drink, in the middle of the gold coins.
» Use the green whipped cream to cover the cone in circular motions.
» Decorate the cone using the red crispy m&ms and Maltesers.
» Place the chocolate star on top of cone and dust your tree with icing sugar.
» Serve immediately and enjoy!

• My Kind of Kool •

Shake ingredients:

1 packet Kinder Bueno
2 Kinder chocolate bars
1 tbsp Nutella
2 pumps chocolate syrup
3 scoops vanilla ice cream
200ml (7fl oz) milk

For presentation:

1 chocolate rimmed glass
1 long straw
whipped cream
$^1/_2$ Kinder Surprise Egg
$^1/_2$ Kinder Bueno bar
1 small piece of Kinder
    chocolate bar

5 skinless roasted
    hazelnuts
3 Maltesers
1 chocolate flake, crushed

Method:

» Place all the ingredients in a blender
   and mix until well combined.

Decorate:

» Before pouring the mixture into the
   glass, create a chocolate rim around
   the top of the glass (see page 13)
» Pour in the blended mixture until it
   reaches the bottom of the rim.
» Place a straw at back towards the left
   of the glass.
» Fill remaining space in the glass with
   whipped cream until it reaches the top
   of the rim.
» Place half of the Kinder Surprise Egg
   on the right, front side of straw.

» On the left side of straw, place the
   Kinder chocolate bar, and the Kinder
   Bueno slight in front of it.
» Create a rim of skinless roasted
   hazelnuts from the Kinder Bueno bar
   to the Kinder Surprise Egg.
» Place three Maltesers inside the
   Kinder Surprise Egg and finish by
   sprinkling the crushed chocolate flake
   over the drink.
» Serve immediately and enjoy!

• Terry and Sue •

Shake ingredients:

whipped cream
2 sponge fingers
100ml (3fl oz) milk
1 tsp coffee

3 Maltesers
icing sugar, sifted

For presentation:

1 chocolate rimmed glass
1 long straw
1 plastic food syringe
1 long dessert spoon

Method:

» Chop the sponge fingers in half and place into the chocolate rimmed glass.
» Place a long spoon and straw into the glass and pour in the milk.

Decorate:

» Fill the syringe with coffee.
» Place a small amount of whipped cream and Maltesers into a small bowl.
» Place the glass, bowl and syringe onto a serving board to serve.
» Serve immediately and enjoy!

GLOSSARY OF TREATS

While some of these treats can be difficult to find, all can be found in international supermarkets, or sweets stores.

Iced VoVo – Similar to a Mikado biscuit in the UK, this treat is a biscuit (cookie) layered with marshallows, strawberry jam and desiccated coconut

Maltesers – Maltesers are small chocolate balls filled with a malt honeycomb center.

Flake – Flakes are a thin chocolate bar made up of thin layers of rolled chocolate.

Tim Tam – Tim Tams are a popular chocolate biscuit (cookie) made of two layers of chocolate biscuit (cookie) separated by a light chocolate cream filling and coated in chocolate.

Oreo – Oreos are a sandwich cookie consisting of two chocolate cookies with a sweet crème filling.

Crunchie – A chocolate bar filled with honeycomb toffee sugar.

Jubes – A jelly candy coated in sugar.

Milky Way – Similar to a Mars Bar, a Milky Way is made of chocolate malt nougat, coated with caramel and chocolate.

Nutella – A hazelnut spread, commonly found in all supermarkets.

Strawberry Clouds – a red, cloud shaped soft candy, strawberry flavored.

Sour Strips (strawberry and bubblegum) – strips of sour and gummy strawberry or bubblegum flavored candy.

Kinder Bueno – a light chocolate bar with a creamy hazelnut center and crispy wafer coated in chocolate.

Kinder Surprise Egg – a small, hollow chocolate egg filled with a small toy.

Ovalteenies – Ovalteenies are round sweets made of compressed Ovaltine, which is a chocolate milk flavoring product made from malt extract.

Pocky Sticks – A popular Japanese snack food that can be bought in supermarkets. Pocky Sticks are chocolate coated biscuit sticks.

Sour Worms – A small gummy candy shaped like a worm. Often come in bright colors and are coated in sugar.

Rice Bubbles (Rice Krispies) – a popular cereal made from crisped rice.

Reese's Pieces – a peanut butter candy, colored orange, yellow and brown.

Strawberries and Cream – a small gummi candy with a white base and red top, to look like a strawberry on top of cream.

Gummi Bears – a small fruit gum candy, similar to jelly babies.

Musk Stick – a small semi-soft pink stick with a musk taste and smell.
Banana lollies (candies) – a small, yellow banana shaped candies. Can be bought from candy stores.

Jersey Caramels –a small, square shaped caramel flavored candy.

Monte Carlo – a sweet biscuit (cookie) made of golden syrup, honey and coconut biscuits (cookies) and filled with vanilla cream and raspberry jam.

Ginger Kisses – a sweet ginger cookie filled with butter cream.

Milo – a chocolate and malt powder to be mixed with milk or water to create a chocolate drink.

Wagon Wheels – a sweet sandwich cookie filled with marshmallow and coated in chocolate.

Index

B
Bang Bang Meringue   80
Billy Bonka   60
Brittany's Musketeers   66
Bueno Mars   52

C
Chainana   22
Chocolate milkshake   34
Coachella   58
Creaming Soda Spider   84
Crunchie Kisses   32
Custarted   92

D
Decorating your glass   13
Double Decker   44

F
Fairies Dream   76
Fifi's Fairy Tale   98

G
Glossary   108

H
Hubba Hubba – 78

I
Iced chocolate   50
Infamous Nutella Milkshake   90
Infamous Peanut Butter Milkshake   94

J
Jenga   54

M
Magic doodle   42
Malt my heart   36
Man-go-crazy   24
Maybe it's Maple   74
Mc'Mazing   48
Mixed berry smoothie   28
Mocha Madness   38
My Kind of Kool   104

N
Notes about safety   11

P
Pash me   18
Peach as bro   16
Peachy mango   20
Pina colada   26
Pink Lady   86

S
Salty Knickers   40

T
Terry and Sue   106
The Hike   70
TVC Tree   100
Twerk it   56

V
Vivo la Vogue   64

W
Wheel of Fortune   96

Acknowledgements

Thank you from Matthew, Sarah and Brendan to all our loyal customers and followers for being a part of The Vogue Café's Decadent Shake journey. Your support makes the café what it is and gives us this great and wonderful opportunity of making a book which we can share with you.

Big shout out to Marcel, Big Pappa, Lynette, Big Mumma for the endless and unconditional support they provide. Our partners – Natasha, Omer and Emma for always pushing us to be creative. Our siblings Kristen and George for being our taste testers, and our awesome little kids, who we can't wait to teach all the tricks! To our wonderful and awesome staff, who we really do consider to be apart of our family, thank you for coming to work and giving it your all day in and day out.

Author Bio

Matthew, Sarah and Brendan Aouad are siblings running a family business making the world a happier place one decadent shake at a time. With experience from every facet of a business, each sibling brings an innovative flair to how a small business should be run and shakes should be made, creating a sweet rivalry that has turned into some of their finest decadent shakes time after time. Love life!

First published in 2016 by New Holland Publishers Pty Ltd
London • Sydney • Auckland

The Chandlery Unit 704, 50 Westminster Bridge Road, London SE1 7QY, United Kingdom
1/66 Gibbes Street, Chatswood, NSW 2067, Australia
5/39 Woodside Ave, Northcote, Auckland 0627, New Zealand

www.newhollandpublishers.com

A record of this book is held at the British Library and the National Library of Australia.

ISBN 9781742578699

Managing Director: Fiona Schultz
Publisher: Diane Ward
Project Editor: Jessica McNamara
Designer: Lorena Susak
Photographer: Sue Stubbs
Production Director: James Mills-Hicks
Printer: Times International Printing, Malaysia

10 9 8 7 6 5 4 3 2 1

Keep up with New Holland Publishers on Facebook
www.facebook.com/NewHollandPublishers